Globe
Advertiser. EST'D 1797.
NEWSPAPER.

SEPTEMBER 29, 1909.

S ROUNDS LIBERTY STATU
DIRIGIBLES OFF FOR AL

BEFORE THE START

**Dayton Man Makes a Tr
Miles at an Elevation c
and Thousands Are Th
He Swoops Along 25
Castle Williams—Carries
pended to His Machine.**

CURTISS MAKES A "JU
OF A QUARTER C

**Ferryboats Stop to Let Their Pa
the Spectacle, and a Choru
From River Craft Greets t
Both Machines Work Well in
—An Ideal Day for Flying.**

To my grandchildren, Felix, Graham, Evan, and Lulu—with much love
— R. B.

To David McCullough
— W. M.

Special thanks to Stephanie Bange,
former librarian at Wright State University

Henry Holt and Company, *Publishers since 1866*
Henry Holt® is a registered trademark of Macmillan Publishing Group, LLC
120 Broadway, New York, NY 10271 • mackids.com

Text copyright © 2021 by Robert Burleigh
Illustrations copyright © 2021 by Wendell Minor
All rights reserved.

Library of Congress Cataloging-in-Publication Data

Names: Burleigh, Robert, author. | Minor, Wendell, illustrator.
Title: Wilbur Wright meets Lady Liberty / Robert Burleigh ; illustrations by Wendell Minor.
Description: New York : Henry Holt and Company, [2021] | "Christy Ottaviano Books." | Includes bibliographical references. | Audience: Ages 5–9
Audience: Grades 2–3 | Summary: "Two American icons meet in this
nonfiction picture book that tells the dramatic true tale of Wilbur Wright's flight circling the Statue of Liberty"–Provided by publisher.

Identifiers: LCCN 2020020578 | ISBN 9781627793681 (hardcover)
Subjects: LCSH: Wright, Orville, 1871–1948–Travel–New York (State)–New York–Juvenile literature. | Aeronautics–Flights–History–20th century
Juvenile literature. Classification: LCC TL540.W7 B8722 2021 | DDC 629.130092–dc23
LC record available at https://lccn.loc.gov/2020020578

Our books may be purchased in bulk for promotional, educational, or business use.
Please contact your local bookseller or the Macmillan Corporate and Premium Sales Department
at (800) 221-7945 ext. 5442 or by email at MacmillanSpecialMarkets@macmillan.com.

First edition, 2021 / Design by John Daly
The artist used gouache watercolor on Strathmore 500 Bristol paper to create the illustrations for this book.
Printed in China by RR Donnelley Asia Printing Solutions Ltd., Dongguan City, Guangdong Province.

1 3 5 7 9 10 8 6 4 2

WILBUR WRIGHT MEETS LADY LIBERTY

ROBERT BURLEIGH

illustrations by
WENDELL MINOR

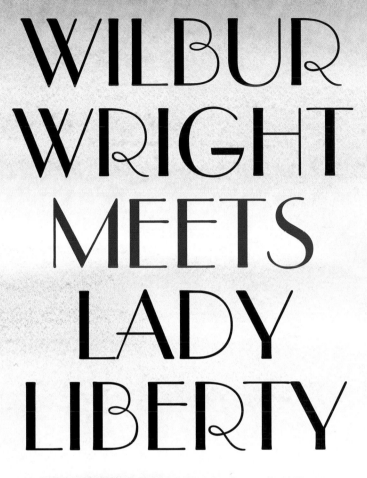

Christy Ottaviano Books

HENRY HOLT AND COMPANY • New York

It won't work! This guy Wilbur Wright must be out of his mind!

I'll believe it only when I see it!

What will people dream up next? Flying to the moon?

Hold on. The signal flags are up. He's about to start.

Can he, Papa? Fly? Really fly in the air?

Let's watch, Juan. Let's watch.

Across the water, Wilbur Wright stands alongside his Wright Flyer, ready to go. He is confident, as always, but at the same time careful. He has even attached a red canoe to the bottom of his plane—just in case!

For a final moment, Wilbur looks out across the water. He sees hundreds of brightly colored ships in the harbor: sailboats, tugboats, ferryboats, rowboats, yachts—even a few navy battleships. And larger than any of them is the luxury liner *Lusitania*, with its great smokestacks giving off dark gray puffs.

Waiting.

And Wilbur sees something else. Across the harbor, near its western edge, the Statue of Liberty shimmers in the morning light. Her torch rises high into the air. Is Lady Liberty calling out, too?

Is she also waiting — for Wilbur Wright?

Even newspaper reporters, held back from the plane by a long rope, are gathered here. A few take pictures, while some call out words of encouragement. But others wonder: Has this man—dressed like an ordinary office worker, with his high, stiff collar, his tie, his vest, his clean business suit—really invented a machine that can fly? And what about the red canoe attached to the bottom of the machine? If Wilbur Wright thinks he can fly his aeroplane, why does he need a rescue boat?

Chattering voices surround Wilbur, yet nothing matters to him now but his flight.

READY! GET SET!

The Wright Flyer, its propellers spinning, rolls down a monorail to build speed for the launch. Wilbur feels the plane suddenly lift, and the land beneath him seems to fall away.

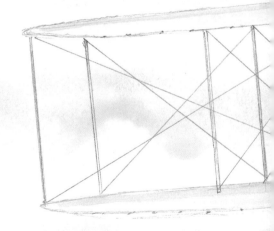

The Flyer angles upward into the air: Ten feet.
Thirty feet. Fifty! From somewhere, a sound
rises — a tidal wave of *ahhs* and *ohhs*.

He's up. He's really in the air!

For now, maybe, but not for long!

To me, it looks like a great big runaway kite.

No, more like a giant spider—with four wings!

He's flying, Papa, he's flying. Where is he going?

Keep watching, Juan. Keep watching.

The Wright Flyer is one hundred feet in the air now. For a moment, Wilbur feels he is in another world. In a quick over-the-shoulder glance, he sees the great city of New York: the tall buildings, the green parks, the wide roadways, the narrow streets dotted with tiny people, strollers, buggies, and carts.

But he leaves all that behind him. Today Wilbur Wright is going to "meet" Lady Liberty!

Wilbur feels the wind rushing past his face. His feet brace on the narrow foot-bar. His grip tightens around the hand levers.

As he flies toward the statue, it slowly becomes larger. And larger. Wilbur takes in everything: Lady Liberty's immense size, the folds in her copper-green robes, the tablet tightly clutched in her left hand, and always, the long right arm raised toward the sky.

Closer. Closer. High above Wilbur Wright is the great statue's face, with its firm gaze that looks out over the harbor. And higher still, above everything, is the gold-tipped torch that seems to call out: *Welcome, you who enter here! Look upon the symbol of America and be free.*

Where is he? I can't see him anymore!

He's out of sight.

I think he crashed!

*No, maybe he's behind the statue,
flying around it?*

Papa, I can't see him.

Now comes the hard part! Carefully, Wilbur banks the
Flyer down and around to his left. The airplane begins
to curve in an ever-tightening circle. Wilbur, cautiously
looking both sideways and ahead, begins to fly past the
statue's waist. For one brief moment, he flies through
shadow. Lady Liberty's huge body seems to block the light.

Careful! Is the Flyer too close? Wilbur hears the roar of alarmed voices — a roller coaster of cries. He understands so well: If even one tip of the Flyer's wing touches the statue, he will spin crazily out of control and plunge to his death.

Concentration is everything. Wilbur leans into the direction of each careful turn. There is only the pilot, the plane, and the enormous figure beside them—so nearby he almost feels he could reach out and touch her gown. He squints, holds fast, and suddenly sweeps back into the bright morning, wide and clear . . . and into a symphony of wild celebration.

From far below, a thunderous cheering rises, falls, and rises again. Flags flutter. Hats fly skyward. Whistles sound. Horns blare.

Passengers crowd the deck of the *Lusitania*, looking up and calling out. Wilbur dips one wing in a playful hello and flies on. The powerful, deep blast from the great ship's foghorn even makes the Flyer shake slightly!

Sailors on the deck of a battleship salute. A lone rower
stands awkwardly in his rowboat and waves. And a
single seagull flaps overhead, startled by the sudden
appearance of this strange double-winged bird.

Wilbur feels as if he and his Wright Flyer are one. He lets out a long breath. The *hoorah*s of triumph fall over him like warm rain. He belongs to this vast gathering of people. And they belong to him.

Aiming toward the island again, he begins to bring the Flyer down. Lower. Lower. Lower. He is free-floating now, until, with a soft *bump-bump*, he is on the sandy ground — in a perfect landing.

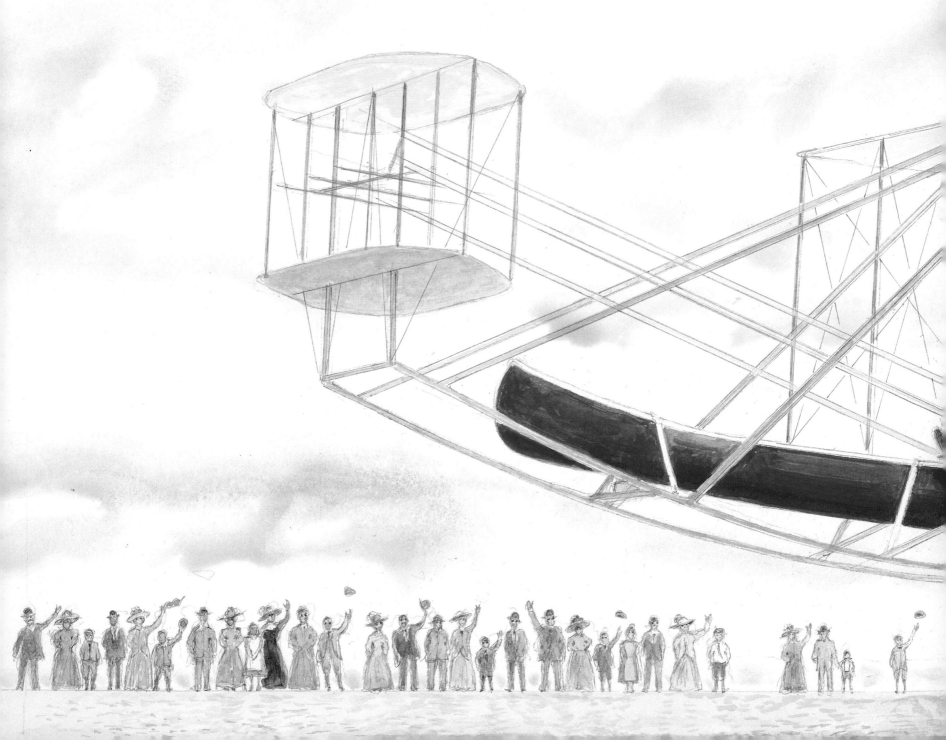

The reporters and news photographers scurry toward him. Wilbur patiently answers their questions. He brushes the dust from one sleeve of his suit coat, smiling into the eye of a clicking camera. Tomorrow he will be on the front page of every newspaper in the city of New York!

The Globe
AND Commercial Advertiser. EST'D 1797.
NEW YORK'S OLDEST NEWSPAPER.
HOME EDITION
WITH LATE AFTERNOON NEWS
ONE CENT

NEW YORK, WEDNESDAY, SEPTEMBER 29, 1909.

WRIGHT IN DARING FLIGHTS ROUNDS LIBERTY STATUE; CURTISS ALSO OUT; DIRIGIBLES OFF FOR ALBANY

WILBUR WRIGHT FLYING OVER THE BAY AND JUST BEFORE THE START

Dayton Man Makes a Trip of Two Miles at an Elevation of 150 Feet and Thousands Are Thrilled When He Swoops Along 25 Feet Above Castle Williams—Carries Canoe Suspended to His Machine.

CURTISS MAKES A "JUMP" OF A QUARTER OF A M

Ferryboats Stop to Let Their Passengers See the Spectacle, and a Chorus of From River Craft Greets the A Both Machines Work Well in Stro —An Ideal Day for Flying.

HALF MOON

The reporters finally hurry off with
their stories. For a brief moment, Wilbur Wright
thinks back. Ten years flash by in his mind: The
first gliders over the sands at Kitty Hawk. The first
takeoff. The first ride in the air. All the slow, hard
progress that has led to this day — this special day.

For one last time, he listens to the distant cheering,
now just a gentle hum . . .

Like I said—easy as pie.

You didn't say that at first! You thought he'd be in the water in a minute!

They say he's flying again tomorrow—down the Hudson River to 125th Street.

And believe me, I'll be watching from my roof!

Papa, Papa—I want to fly an aeroplane when I grow up. Can I?

Of course, Juan. This is America. And everything is possible.

AUTHOR'S NOTE

Into the Air — Maybe!

The story of brothers Wilbur and Orville Wright, and their invention of the airplane (once spelled "aeroplane"), is a story filled with determination, scientific study, hard work, and courage.

Wilbur (born April 16, 1867) and Orville (born August 19, 1871) grew up mostly in Dayton, Ohio. As young men they started several businesses, including a print shop and a bicycle shop. It was at this time that they turned their attention to flight. Was it possible to build a heavier-than-air machine that could lift itself and its pilot off the ground and venture into the sky? To most people, the idea seemed utterly absurd. But Wilbur and Orville decided to find out for themselves.

Over the next few years (1900-1903), they experimented with a variety of gliders and kite-like devices. Slowly, they began to solve the problems of wing size and shape, propeller size and angle, the position of the pilot, controls for the plane, and the kind of engine needed to propel the plane through the air. They read books, experimented in their bike shop, and traveled each year to a windy beach area near Kitty Hawk, North Carolina, to test their machine.

The great breakthrough occurred at Kitty Hawk on December 17, 1903. Taking turns in their most recently improved glider-plane, now called the Flyer, the brothers took to the air, one at a time. Orville went first (for 12 seconds); later that day Wilbur flew long enough (59 seconds) and with enough control to realize that flight was indeed possible. Their simple telegram home — sent the same day — said in part: "Success . . . started from Level with engine power alone."

September 29, 1909: Look Up, America!

It was 1909, and few Americans had seen a plane in the air. At the same time, New York City was planning a huge celebration to commemorate scientific and technological advances during the city's history, including Robert Fulton's 1807 steamboat service up and down the Hudson River. As part of this, the Wright brothers were invited to exhibit their new Flyer. They accepted the invitation to make two flights. The first was to take place over New York Harbor on September 29; the second—a few days later—was to be a longer flight down the Hudson. These flights, both executed by Wilbur, were the Wrights' first public exhibitions in the United States. Thousands of Americans—many of whom were doubters—came to watch. The unqualified success of the two flights did much to bring aviation to America's attention and led to the further development of aviation everywhere.

Some Interesting Facts About the Wright Brothers and the New York Flights

- The Wright brothers were brave—but they were also cautious. They made it a rule that they would never be up in the same plane at the same time. This way, if a plane crashed and one of the brothers died, the other would be able to carry on their work.

- The Wrights were not the only people working to develop a heavier-than-air flying machine. In fact, another inventor had attempted to take to the air just nine days before the Wrights' first successful flight. But Samuel P. Langley's machine, attempting to take off from a houseboat, merely plopped into the river!

- Wilbur's New York Harbor flight was the first either of the brothers had made over a body of water.

- Meanwhile, Orville was busy, too! During the summer and fall of 1909, he was in Germany giving flying demonstrations before large crowds including German royalty and important military officials.

- Wilbur did not live long after he became famous—but his death was not due to an airplane accident. He died at age forty-five on May 30, 1912, from typhoid fever.

- Orville Wright outlived his brother by almost forty years. Orville, who lived to see many important changes in aviation, died on January 30, 1948.

- Many people were at first skeptical of the Wright brothers' claim to have invented a flying machine. Before the brothers convinced the French, some newspapers in Paris called them *bluffeurs*, or "bluffers."

- The Statue of Liberty was unveiled in 1886 on Bedloe's Island (now Liberty Island) in New York Harbor. It was placed at this spot so that ships coming to New York would pass it as they arrived.

- How tall is the Statue of Liberty? The statue itself is just over 150 feet. And the base is the same height. That's a total of slightly more than 300 feet — or around thirty stories tall!

- The tablet in Lady Liberty's left hand represents the law. The date of American independence is inscribed on the tablet: JULY IV MDCCLXXVI (July 4, 1776).

- One of the many spectators at Wilbur Wright's New York Harbor flight exhibition was ten-year-old Juan Trippe, the "Juan" shown in this story. Young Juan's excitement at the event inspired him to become an aviator — and later to found Pan American (Pan Am) Airways!

- The Wright Brothers were also excellent photographers. They photographed their work step-by-step along the way. In fact, their achievement is one of the most carefully documented inventions in human history.

- The great luxury liner *Lusitania* went on to suffer a cruel fate during World War I. On May 7, 1915, it was torpedoed by a German U-boat off the southern coast of Ireland. Of the 1,962 passengers and crew aboard the *Lusitania* at the time of the sinking, 1,197 lost their lives.

ILLUSTRATOR'S NOTE

The torch of Frédéric-Auguste Bartholdi's Statue of Liberty has changed three times since 1886, the year the statue was dedicated. Before the dedication, the U.S. Light-House Board cut a double row of staggered holes for electric lights inside the flame. In 1892, the upper row of holes was replaced by a band of windows around the flame. Since I found no photographic reference for the 1892 version of the flame, I chose the more familiar version, done in 1916 by Gutzon Borglum. Borglum's version of the torch is now on display in the Statue of Liberty Museum. The final version of the torch was installed in 1985 with a replica of Bartholdi's original design. Covered in gold, it shines brightly in the sun and glows in the spotlights at night.

Bibliography

Crouch, Tom D. *The Bishop's Boys: A Life of Wilbur and Orville Wright.* New York: W. W. Norton and Company, 1989.

Heppenheimer, T. A. *First Flight: The Wright Brothers and the Invention of the Airplane.* Hoboken, NJ: John Wiley & Sons, 2003.

Howard, Fred. *Wilbur and Orville: A Biography of the Wright Brothers.* New York: Ballantine, 1988. (Republished by Dover Publications, Mineola, New York, 1998.)

McCullough, David. *The Wright Brothers.* New York: Simon & Schuster, 2015.

FOR YOUNGER READERS

Freedman, Russell. *The Wright Brothers: How They Invented the Airplane.* New York: Holiday House, 1991.

Krensky, Stephen. *Taking Flight: The Story of the Wright Brothers.* New York: Simon & Schuster, 2000. (Aladdin Paperbacks edition.)

Parker, Steve. *The Wright Brothers and Aviation.* London: Belitha Press, 1994. (Republished by Chelsea House Publishers, New York and Philadelphia, 1995.)

Quote Source

"Success . . . started from Level with engine power alone." World Digital Library, wdl.org/en/item/11372.

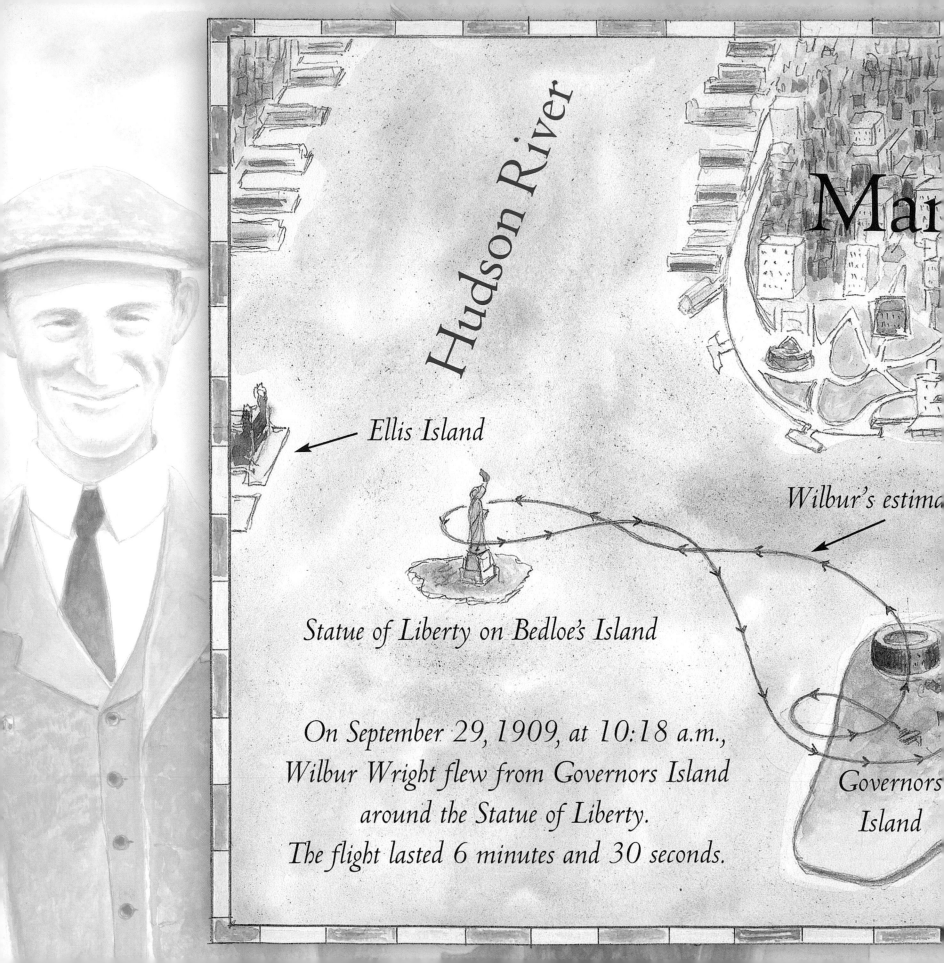

Hudson River

Ma[r]

Ellis Island

Wilbur's estima[te]

Statue of Liberty on Bedloe's Island

Governors
Island

On September 29, 1909, at 10:18 a.m.,
Wilbur Wright flew from Governors Island
around the Statue of Liberty.
The flight lasted 6 minutes and 30 seconds.